Frost on the Van

By Cameron Macintosh

"Quick, Jen!" said Mum.
"We must go!
You will miss the camp bus!"

"I have lost my hat!"
said Jen.

"Is a hat on your camp list?"
said Mum.

"Yes!" said Jen.

"It's in the van!" yelled Mum.

The van was in thick mist.

It had lots of frost on it.

"It's such thick frost,"
said Mum.
"I can not get it off!"

"This is not the best luck,"
said Jen.

"We must wet the van,"
said Mum.

"I will fill a big jug!"
yelled Jen.

Jen ran back to tip the jug
on the frost.

The frost got wet
and ran down the van.

"The frost is off!" Jen said.

"You did the best job!"
said Mum.

"Have you got all the things on your list?" said Mum.

"Yes!" said Jen.

"Then let's go!" said Mum.

CHECKING FOR MEANING

1. What couldn't Jen find at the start of the story? *(Literal)*

2. What did Jen do to get the frost off the van? *(Literal)*

3. In what season of the year does this story take place? *(Inferential)*

EXTENDING VOCABULARY

must	What does the word *must* mean? Does it mean you can, or you have to?
lost	What does it mean if something or someone is *lost*? What should you do?
mist	What is another word that has a similar meaning to *mist*? E.g. fog. What is it like to walk in the mist? What happens to your clothes?

MOVING BEYOND THE TEXT

1. What is a camp list? Why do you think schools give children a list of things to take on school camp?

2. Discuss the other items that would have been on Jen's camp list.

3. Have you been on a school camp? What did you do? What did you enjoy most?

4. Have you ever had frost on your car or van? What did you do?

SPEED SOUNDS

| ft | mp | nd | nk | st |

PRACTICE WORDS

camp

must

lost

list

mist

frost

and

best